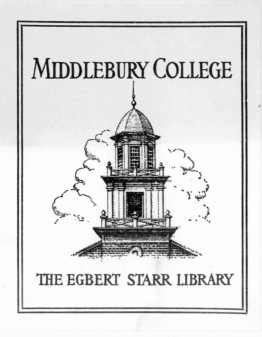

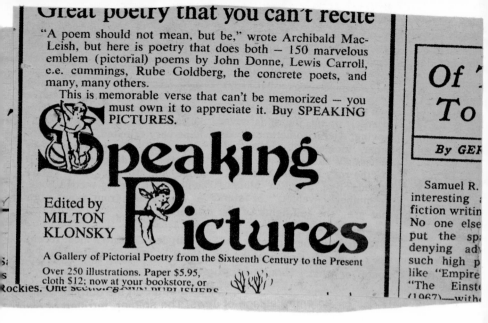

Of
To

By GE

Samuel R.
interesting
fiction writin
No one else
put the spa
denying adv
such high p
like "Empire
"The Einst
(1967)—with

First winner of the Walt Whitman
Award sponsored by the Academy
of American Poets. 1975

1st book
20/

Climbing
Into the Roots

Winner of The Walt Whitman Award for 1975

Sponsored by the Academy of American Poets and supported by the Copernicus Society of America, the Walt Whitman Award is given annually to the winner of an open competition among American poets who have not yet published their first books of poetry. Judge for 1975: William Meredith.

Climbing
Into the Roots

Reg Saner

HARPER & ROW, PUBLISHERS
New York, Evanston, San Francisco, London

The author wishes to thank the University of Colorado
Council on Research and Creative Work for the Fellowship
year during which part of these poems were written.

Grateful acknowledgment is made to the following
magazines in which some of the poems first appeared:
*The Carleton Miscellany, The Colorado Quarterly,
Epoch, Epos, The Little Magazine, The Living
Wilderness, The Malahat Review, The Ohio Review,
Outerbridge, Perspective, Poet & Critic, Prairie Schooner,
Puerto del Sol, The Small Pond Magazine, Southern
Poetry Review, Wind Magazine.*

"Camping the Divide," "Indian Peaks Colorado," "How
the Laws of Physics Love Chocolate," and "Cony
Creek" first appeared in *Poetry.*

FIRST EDITION

Designed by Dorothy Schmiderer

Library of Congress Cataloging in Publication Data
Saner, Reg.
  Climbing into the roots.
  I. Title.
PS3569.A5254C6 1976   811'.5'4   75–7953
ISBN 0–06–013762–2
ISBN 0–06–013763–0 pbk.

76 77 78 79 10 9 8 7 6 5 4 3 2 1

To Anne

"In te misericordia, in te pietate, . . . in te s'aduna quantunque in creatura è di bontate."

Contents

III

IV

V

I

Camping the Divide: Indian Peaks, Colorado

1

Refrigerator tropics. Trees thick
as rain. Even the light is sopping.
We climb following a bootlace
stream, creek and waterfall by turns
through forest so dense
the dead spruce can barely topple.
They squeak down, taking years
to hit. Hummocks muzzle windfallen pine
that dissolves in a lard of sponge
stumps and fern swale
deepening the bog-soft ground.
On a log wide as a barge or small
fat ship I straddle and watch the stream
pour by, falling alongside so fast
it's hard to believe we're not
headed to the Divide by water.

2

At timberline we begin hiking
the grand smash and hurl
over a crockery grind of shale—
working up a perfectly useless sweat,
hugging boxcar faults like lovers—
to squirm among
this difficult magnificence
where we are most our own.

3

Here in the havoc country
what's left of trees finishes in talons.
The split sky goes manic, booming
its laundry strangle up down and sideways
at once. Nubbled trunks of Engleman
and fir, wrist-thick, blown bald
as potato skin in front. A bossy
one-way wind unfurling this last, highest
lake. We watch its ice-water chop
jogging in place.

4

To start our freeze-dried hash
I dribble white gas over the windfall
of twigs you've stacked. They jump
my match, a big red-assed bird
phoenixed out of dead sticks.
The rags of flame thrash and split,
with dark gaps
where the wind takes bites.

5

8:30 sundown. Granite swags of blue scarp
turning in the orangeade air. Then
a roseglow, then a red, deep
as the last of our bird's blood fire.
The sky lies down a while.

The lake slows to a stop.
Its scrub of evergreen margins let up
their thick chop and wobble.
We stand to look.
The light makes something else
of Navaho Peak, of Kiowa,
of that Niwot Ridge we'd figured out
to be an Indian mother-god
worn from too many kids.
We feel the light dying in the lake
pull the Divide together.

6

Like the dead we see ourselves
slipping off into the weather. Delicate
flurries of white and whiskery ash
stir from a few red lumps
as the old wind rises again. We stretch
in mummy bags to the chin, timing
our talk to the tent's nylon whip and crackle.
Near the bank where water tongues
try the lips of stones
a gone light winks and paddles,
making wingbeats in our eyes.
We follow it further off
into a mindless applause that carries
and fades—daylight broken into voices,
our hike's big picture breaking
down, its sky blown over the lake's lower
edge and falling apart
into the Valley of the North St. Vrain. ·

Under us all night we hear dark stones
talking over the way we came. And somewhere
far back in our sleep
feel a high river, going home.

Fingerprints

"Good old galactic
Geographic!" Its low speed
four-color presses are orbiting Africa
massively clear: that great green torso,
sand-lion shoulder, potato-clay foot.
My thought threads the needle
of posterity's glass eye
up there somewhere still
ogling round the room
while a figure's edges burn
as he winds, falling into his next shot
like tinfoil molasses in space.
His thick fingers drift my eyes
into focus here on a page.
The French-curve mechanics of fluids,
marbling tremendous weather
out of the same polar storms
that vinyl our bathroom floor.

I imagine I see what I know—
Asia's starling clouds
frozen in swarms. Stadia packed
to gaping with Brazilian oysters
applauding their beach. All heads
that are—hidden here
in the vast winter-color bone game.

My skull's shards seeping apart

like continental plates,
in the city of Boulder at 4 P.M.
December 28, 1975, I fold up
the ten fingerprints of myself
within this beautiful picture of Earth.
Out of a mouth falling secretly
as a world of ears
on microfiche
I say this to snowflakes.

Another Grand Night in the Wide Machine

My favorite stars shiver
like seeds, my brain is Tarzan
and German beer.

To reach the water I park
my white Chevy, carefully setting
the brake—then slide down
a banked sand cliff,
over dunes, past manzanita shadows
heavy as black bear.

An offshore breeze whispers
the odd clumps of cord-grass,
then nearing the edge I feel
the pack of wet sand, hear a broad
difference taking turns.
A lapping. A blue tick tick.

I've nothing whatever in mind
and nothing I can name
has gathered me here to become
all the animals under the moon,
our simple faces tilted; poised
at the moon's salt lick.

Cony Creek

Along the spit and slap and musical
parachute of Cony Creek
I guess at 7 miles more
down trail to the car. Wind, sea-green,
splits to an idiot crowd chasing itself
over Snowbank Lake. In warps
and grovels these timberline fir
live on their knees to its weather.

Up here the other weather is rock.
Each minor ridge slabbed with trivia
20 feet thick makes me immense
and nil wherever I look.
Watching it holocaust, I rub
my mind on the stone.

Mountains blow out of the ground
millennial inch by inch.
Goats in their high-heeled shoes
nibble common prairie flowers, riding them
all the way to the top.
Eons to adapt.

Settling my pack's aluminum frame
I nap. For 45 minutes,
maybe an hour, the only sound—this wind
carrying smooth as alluvial dimes
while centuries off in my bones
a granite flute practices notes.

How the Laws of Physics Love Chocolate!

1

This dumbbell bee must be working
the half-dozen highest buttercups on earth.
Low alpine sun, bright enough to hurt.
Under my feet a 7-acre snowbank gargles
like gangster summer, riddled with kitchen taps.
Folding the map to a hat I squint under its brim
at the bee that can't get enough.
Corollas needlepoint moss. Way above
timberline and the tundra still corny
with blossom. Each cliff face, the same
machine of prey, able to wipe my brains
on its next stone. I come because
the useless is pure Greek.
At the back of each columbine's head,
a consort of blue trombones.

2

The typical sublime of these glacial valleys!
Their sky a bag of snakes, their wind
the usual life of crime. Terrain
as if gravity always won. This depth
sensed under my boots—not all
snow's an orchard flowing south.
A crater lake the map finds
too small for a name, ice-banked
800 feet down. Clear edges darkened

to bottled dye toward the center.
My first longest throws won't reach,
then the splashed rock—waffling under water
blue-green as Engleman spruce.
A climber fallen and slowly turning
in this bad dream, beautiful
beyond my knowing how, its slash of bubble
threading the inner ear.

3

Holding hands with a driven bee,
surveying granite weather. Due east,
racks of cumulus scud the plains
like garlands of hot cream. Day sets.
Distant strip-farms of wheat
go blood ripe, then one dusk bruise.
The miles of braided stream, Jasper Creek
panicked half a degree from ice.
A country saves what's worthless for last.
Climbing down to the tent, twilight
should be enough. Marmots squeaking
like birds. The wildflower stars.
These priceless leavings we now
call wilderness.

4

Sunset over brute force. Yes,
"War is the father of all"; and "Everything
moves through everything else."
At last, Heraclitus, we two are alone.

"That simply amazing rock on which you sat—
admit it was this rock." After 25
hundred years I know Heraclitus
is not even dust. And that he agrees.
Together we praise
the intelligence of fire, staring out
into every distance there is.

October Rolleicord

for Ron Billingsley

Across Glacier Gorge
my blue eye
riding the fine, ball-bearing silk
of good German work. Log
and windfall foregrounds
I crop, adjust,
don't take. Calendar art
at the edge of winter,
this aspen fire
the great perennial
too gorgeously banal to shoot.

Surface froth on a stream's
black-water pools. Wide-angle droplets
on twigs. The way
their sky's in a hurry
yet held.

Each film changed for sun
higher up, the Verichrome rolls
vacuum-sealed,
yellow bolsters sliding
fatter out of each box.

Twisting my macro-lens
into a particular aspen fleck
fallen vein side up. Then

narrowing down
till depth of field
becomes one of five
water beads
with a mountain
looking into its leaf.

October all afternoon. This light
holding apple-crisp. My finger
and thumbnail on the last
plump roll, breaking
the seal. Hearing it gasp.

Three

So quiet. As if everything here
had happened forever. Ron at the water's
other end, his down jacket a splurge
of orange, staring through blind
mica windows in slabs, its slag wreckage
broad as a warehouse wall. On alpine plush
I loll, quizzing a low knot of sunflowers
eons have dwarfed. Not one petal
stirs. There is absolutely nothing
to hear. Even the scrappy lake
gone calm, an island of twilight.
Above a tent whose blue slack
neither ripples nor furls,
Dick sits looking down, looking up.
Three who do nothing but listen.
This tongue we've brought with, and left.
Like a silence coming out of the stones,
the universe flying at terrible speeds
further into itself.
If it is not here it is nowhere.
The stillness where all words are kept.

The Space Eater Camps at Fifth Lake

To make this scene I climb miles
upgrade on my knees
taking things in. The downhill water
bright at the seams, tossed salad swatches
of trail, deer dung gumballing
the ground. Each sawn trunk of windfall,
a birthday surrounded, its bull's-eye
rippling from seed
like a stone in the lake. At ponds
whose tundra edges seem rich
I put my hand on Miss America's muff.

Packing in, I've time to think
how silly I look, lugging all this metaphor,
but make camp. My thoughts squat
their twig fire like city wolves,
as under these great magma winds
we play Rousseau
lounging his garden bench at Versailles,
prying the lid of primitive time
rational as topiary. There can be
no real loneliness here; I marrow it
into each crag.

Towards midnight I crawl from the tent
to watch a moon nearly at full
pulled from my own sublime,
its grand gesture

stuffing the mountain's ark
with shadows. Further up, this galaxy
I forgot gives my eyes
both barrels.

Under the rosy foreskin of dawn,
turned for a parting glance, I leave
and take all I can. The mountain's huge
bite of glacial cirque
hovers, a small glass square
pressed to the shape of a tent,
with, still slightly warm,
a sleep-print. All summer I'll come
and go, eating spaces like these
to make sure.
My death must be a simply enormous death.

II

Climbing Into the Roots

The divide's revolving door of cloud
and waterfall. Tundra's autumnal crackle.
This air-tunnel topiary—kinnikinnick's
evergreen flow, surviving only in the lee
of rocks. Is the human wind-simple
as that? Anne home, tucking Nick in,
then Tim, wishing me down.
The more she aches to hear "if this got lost
my breath would cut ten leagues below
the earth," the more I can't.

7:15, and my wristwatch stealing
everything in sight. On upslope air
a down-vested arctic bird, junco I think,
full stretch and motionless, sunset
lining its wings. Miles from talk
these chatty hikers overheard
aren't there. Runoff's roar and fade
accordions across Sprague gorge
where the drop's a cool
900 feet. Out of that, my ventriloquist ear
fakes the high-speed flush of tires
through a kitchen window. Anne there
sipping her nightcap cigarette.

The thin bell of a Sierra cup. Booted
gravel, or a cough—missing speakers
drawn to the tent. Up where the gone

is real I catch myself catching
the simplest things from rocks so dumb
they echo only one-syllable names.
Beyond the voices of bootprints even,
I hear how much voices count.
But Anne, I'm still retarded.
After 2 days traveling hard with both hands
on a wind whose name in one tongue
is *stone, sand* in another, how can I say
what it's like, coming that much closer
to home? Or how strange,
climbing so far alone
into these roots where we touch.

Hiking at Night

The feet go blind,
bang around a lot but
like playing at death
it's fun.
The dry static
of twigs, the inkblot
underbrush,
the wind
not quite intelligible
but in it with other
animal sounds.

That boy scientist
ahead on the trail, manning
his bicycle pump,
injecting this night ladder
of roots with my classic
fear of snakes.

On the edges of trees
occasional darklings
perched,
calling each other
like air that I eat up.

A cool night sky,
my future falling away
both sides.

My headstart dad
the famous tireless skindiver
getting there,
keeping pace
just underneath.

Stoning the River

My caveman stance and grunt
on the bank, prying
a rock with heft enough.
The windshield broken,
my broken face
blown through.

Standing clear.
Hearing the mind flush,

feeling the light
pull back together,

the river heal.

Clouds like Swedish Blondes

Tunneled from work on my future
I blink to see
how it must have been all day.
Clean as a spoon the cross-lit air,
and neighborhood columbine
exposing their beautiful genitals.
A blue-haired poodle—Poston's
I think—trotting round
taking evening in by nose.
Over the valley I glance for miles
under clouds like Swedish blondes
in mulberry velvet. Twigged
in Chaney's pin oak, a nuthatch
small as my thumb gets off
trills and pipsqueaks
while, through preen oil
along the neck, I look into the oak's
green and iridescent sky.
His head cocks.
The evening barely moves.
Together we listen
for the rest of his story.
Common summer, and simply this life
if we'd let it.

Above Timberline

Over the bare lake,
starlight the only weather, our fire
the final tree. Through boot soles
we follow its sunworks, a ruddy plum
shriveling quietly back
to the roots. We stare by turns
down at embers, up among
the brilliant hieroglyphs. Our eyes
spider light-years, webbing star
to star. "Who was first
to draw these lines? Everyone?
Everyone who's looked?"

Below the great crag blackout
of Indian Peaks our pupils widen
at darkness tucking stones
into one another's arms.

So quiet. We forget
about breath
till we hear belt leather creak.
To make talk, we listen.

That enormous reach
cupped beyond the Dipper puts
its shell to the ear. A steady
crush and uncrumple of wet red
silk . . . a bloodstream

. . . ours, counting
on its fingers. What it has lost
in coming so far.
What bones it has driven, nailing
this earth together.

Night of the Big Chinook

Way up I feel the huge
and violent dead, defunct stars
riding a sky blown clean,
nailing into the mind
out of a void
it breaks my teeth to think—
as under an ice hunk of a moon
I stagger into gusts whose whiplash
pops my nylon hood like a saddle.
On a whim, yammering out
Old Testament scraps
recalled off the first page
just to hear this great wind
gibber them back in my face.
Lurching the rip and surf
of black air empty as the absolute
zero of tongues I hear
our deepest boulders creak
and rot, our forests
tearing themselves apart,
our fields
dragging and screaming.

Tasting the Morning Abyss

On the bed's edge
tasting the morning abyss—
the smashed hair,
the stunned blood—as if
I'd been driving alone
all night.
            Kitchen noises.
Cups, spoons.
A refrigerator that sucks
unsealed like a hatch.
In the bathroom
as I lather up
the basin swirls and chokes
its draining water.
The steamed mirror grows
vaguely paternal.

        I'm the absence
about to become a man
I remember, as I remember him
watching him shave.
Looking into the eyes
I hear my father
coughing to me
from the bottom of a river.

The Delicate Breathing of Small Animals

February four o'clock
and our shriveled eyes
peep out. A thin sun
going off on crutches.
The Chinese elm straggles
our brown lawn in warts
and switches. Roots
dive in the earth. With night
coming on a mountain wind
that rises, tottering our
mortgaged house, my empty
blood's turned stray dog
muzzling in a dirty paper cup.

Now if ever
is the time for thinking
on milkweed pods. Bursts
whose soft light can balloon
a field, or recalling
the patience of plain grass
under the snow.
A time for hearing among these black
hulks of mountains
a winter courage
in the delicate breathing
of small animals.

Passing It On

I was three and already
my world shook with you.
Now I'm what's left. The eyes
I have are yours, your mouth.
That trick of your upper lip—
and those slurred 1-syllables
you still slide
into a few of my words.

Now in my dreams again
and again your lacquered
casket sinks, becomes your door
into the grass. To one side
the clay heap waits to fall
a shovelful at a time.

I walk up close. I heft a clod,
then eat. Gnawing, I taste
the darkness between us
you suddenly died in. For years
it's been the red fist
of your heart that I've chewed
and gagged on, till I'm bled out
and odd of it.

And your small, thick hands.
Their anger has made my own hand
tremble, passing it on.

Already I'm hurt
by my son's look—the way
his eyes beat and grow secret
under this strange love
shaken into me.

The Moon

Whether as stone or lady,
whether as a thin blue sleep
over snow hills
or as Helen in Egypt,
whether as vampire-and-werewolf of air
or fire walking the summer water,
your light
has run through all our wars
and always come home.
Old Adam's white rose of time,
promise of that kingdom of light downstream,
lone mare pale against the night shore
and belly-deep in surf.
Earth's moving target of dreams,
its last ditch and springboard,
dirt ivory, deserted fresco, firework and ice.
Skylight of rock anniversaries
falling always in place,
vision and witness, woman and death,
meditative bone beneath the skin.
The poet's and everyman's two-dollar whore,
and the one love
we all waited for
at last descending the staircase.

Just Say Etruscan

. . . and in my head
a crock lip flowers this
shovel edge our tongue
grating down
in a ditch
a workman's clay thumb
squeezing soil clear
of petal forms ensculped
or pressed then fired
like bursts
of tiny spoons
his glance up
into my shadow
our half-smile over
nothing much
a bit more of priceless trash
its twenty-five-century rise
to this better light
meaning us

and if
we stood there first
so what the rare
is everyday as dirt
a word strange red
and common
as burnt clay underfoot
its petals so crude

they can't recall
any one flower I know
just the idea of flowers
meaning all

III

Listening for Indians

We believe we remember the spot. An Indian
lying with his ear to the ground,
his breath no longer real.
Where he kept it we imagine a blood
of arrows sticking through both sides.
Looking closer
we make out trademarks. Browning
Winchester Remington Springfield—
the fine old .30-caliber
Mayflower names.
As for those cave-paintings in his head,
those smokes of earth color—
that one about the deer, that one
about the fish and otter,
the one about the buffalo—
we know they're spent. Gone out.
Know that while there *were* Indians
they were never this Indian,
who was never millions
but one of a reasonable number.
And this soil of earth colors lying over
breath no longer real
was never those cave-paintings—images
out of another country.
         Even so, we go on
imagining ourselves a buckskin man
like a single peaceable nation
finally reading signs
in the eyes of deer, otter, buffalo

long wandered off.
As we cup an ear to the remembered ground
we gentle our breath,
listening for Indians.

One War Is All Wars

"There isn't enough.
Somebody must die for it."

And simply as that
the black rubber bags
zip shut
over the oatmeal brains
over the garbage faces
like official breath.

Line after line after
line regular as
domino theory turned
into dark weather

the white crosses
neat
as the masts of small ships
sailing deep.

Flag

Up from the bottom
of a thick green light
he rises, wearing
his crocodile skin
like a difficult lesson
the river has taught him.

Overhead the cautious
staff members circle.
From time to time
they alight,
picking bits of experience
from his teeth.

As he levels squarely
into the nation's great
glass eye
he is saddened
by the malice of others
but he forgives them,
weeping thumbtacks.

On his right hand
and behind
the flag of his office hangs,
a wet 4th of July,
refusing to burn.

Sod Huts on the Plains near Aurora, Colorado

In our eyes a workhorse wind
blurs the winter sun, makes the far
slope one mousey spillway of weeds.
The ashen growth curls thin
as whittlings underfoot. What'll we plant?

Talking up crops we pay no mind
to the loud air of Stapleton Field
or the unraveled atmosphere
heavy with brief machines. Like good
movie extras we're lost in our parts
behind clodhopper Bible names
and high rawbone cheeks. Calling out
to Rebecca, Abel, Ephraim,
Zebadiah, we let our Adam's apples bob.
But inside? What'll we do
about wall dirt crumbling off sod
stacked up like a closed book?
We hold it with whitewash we've learnt
to stroke broom-thick. We ignore
3 fighter jets fresh up
from their Buckley strip, hustling
the horizon lean level and fast.
We've grown steady as this weather
riding the land, and barely flinch
at hearing the sky get blown
in half. How lumber's skimpy!
We'll have to wagon-haul
each plank two weeks

from the mountains west. Without bushes
or trees we find ourselves stooped
to gathering buffalo dung
that'll heat and bake.

Before driving away
we cramp into a final hut, go through
scarlet fever, childbirth in a mud box.
On the turnpike we can't get over
how recently life out here
was like that, and worse. And how
gain means loss. And how
none of it is us.

For Six Navaho Smoke Jumpers:
Monument Forest, New Mexico

Around its small lake
the field chokes
where six black-haired men stare
at the emotional problems of fire.
It circles their last rock,
which is nothing but water. Near them
the branches slobber
and weep as their clothes
begin to steam like boughs,
while high over fir
and lodge-pole the last of the magpies
flying hard against updraft
can do nothing about it. Tree
after tree bursts
into harvest,
and the wide eyes of the men
understand. In this thick breath
of nails, they wear skins
already captive. Their teeth
will become black
as early rings of stones
in caves. With the next gust
their body hair will curl,
then flash in tongues
teaching them all there is to learn
about seasons. As the forest cools
they will blow like autumn
across America.

Smiling at 180

You hold it floored, between 90/95
never passing the North Platte,
glimpsing where its gone waters stumbled
and graveled among
a rubbage of mudbark willow.

Crows flapping the bare clod fields
in low gusts.
The black road flapping your tires.
The winter sun in husks.

There was a sea here once.

The slow Nebraska prairie heaves
its thick troughs and swells,
shouldering past into a rear view
at the base of your skull.

Suddenly out of the other direction
the right girl comes along fast
barreling her red Camaro—
a friend's sock feet
up and sleeping in back.

You each flick a smile forever
at 180
and split wide open
into a small pair of mirrors.

Palmyra, Illinois in Bug-Time

Like the season itself
the half moon gains weight
under its August haze of sweat.
Across the highway, solid as Pharoah legs
in Egypt, Brohan's Co-op Elevator plumps
the air, all that July wheat
on its grain-sack breath. As the white
customized Merc tears ass,
heading for Kip's Lounge near Table Grove,
its hot backwash slaps my face
with clover surf, fresh cut.
Sloshing the brim,
all the night silences wobble,
recover.

Along its willow edge
our frog crop at Strawn's Creek
begins what's left
of counting on the moon.
I can hear each prosperous frog
wind himself up
like a thick green watch.

IV

Moss Campion as the History of Green

1

this young stream
shelf-to-shelf muttering
itself into beards
a grass pinch
looking out
of its granite crack
for something better
to eat
the windfallen time
thrown up by its roots
my breath caught
on broken staircase terrain
trailing the history
of green like sperm
backpacking
into the womb

2

under gravity's big guns
the body's hunches
the northeast face slab
after slab creviced
and charged
ripe to unload
its gray thornbush of rock
chunks bumping

my head on the pack frame
looking them up
their smash
that earthquakes
the back of the mind
a stampede of beasts
such pure pain
their tremendous
beginning of sand

3

over snowpack's slump
and bowl ringing the eyes
with glare
jamming in each boot
edge after edge
lungs beating out of control
wild as swimmers spent
about to go down
kicking a ladder up here
from zero dunes
where nothing can live one
brown sparrow how small
hopping
like nobody special
pecking the ice
for seeds

4

between slag mountains
their ice lake this lithic
ambush of cliff
higher still
a speck pure black
its single gravelly caw
flagging home
through ruin
and suddenly mist
the rip of gutteral weather
a tufted block
nonetheless
its shaken petals making me look
moss campion i think what
green what tiny
shirt-button blossoms
each calyx's discrete
yet ardent pink
such faith these light
millions of years then
slowly the stone
finding its way
into this

That Line Drawn at the Moon

Home from the lecture's "Electron Escape
among Inter-Galactic Sources"
I relish the chirrup and twirp
of our evening's neighborhood boys
as they hover suppertime
in their bicycle twilight.

The old fir have managed cones
for the new fir, and irrigated strips
of Colorado wheat swag east of town
like harvest time, despite the gravelly soil,
bone-dry air.

All this trafficking between the southern
season, the northern season.
In an hour or two, when the taillights
of the big bang
begin making the darkness clear
I'll be in the yard again for a fresh look.
Staring up between, guessing
how huge a dark we're in.

No wonder medieval man gazed up
as though from the salt cup of the heart
and drew that line at the moon:
flux and dross for a time below,
but a saving clarity
out among the stars. Medieval stars
of course, that seemed to be so.

Isolation Peak, El. 13,118

Deranged, Hitlerian country
faulted with monoliths that glint
of homicidal iron.
Its blocks and cracks obsess.
Crippled faces empty
as God's eye. A pair of raveled
streams, their creek-water clouds
laid out in threads.
Dead breath of jaws.
Locked winds
unable to swerve.
I live here twice on Sundays.

Barnstormer

Even dismissing the annual
offer we feel our skeptical eyes
falling in with gravity's
old soft sell.
The biplane camouflaged
as foliage banking
on air. The stacked pages tossed—
their slipstream bucket of color
slurried and blown wide open.
This proposition that ripples
like water, settling
easy as the mother tongue,
one leaflet at a time.

These tatterdemalion
parachute elms, their messages
drifting so beautifully apart
on our lawns. And our eyes again,
turned into seeing themselves
becoming not quite
what they were. Gently eating
these leaflets months from now
when in fact
we are not even listening.

Fall

oh yes
you could think
an age of gold
the wind among aspen
the light
spoken in tongues

or of
what's ruddy
the apple in eve's eye
adam
biting so deep
he tilts the earth

oh yes
you could think
it goes on
even now
that this sumac
must bleed for it

Tundra at Bighorn Flats

Prostrate winds of gorse. An undulance
stretching miles between steps.
Climbing into it he stares
through everyone he knows, terrible
gray shapes blown beyond language.
Animals and plants growing smaller:
bear into marmot, horses turned mice,
redwoods sunk to lichen blots
pebble-thick over slabs. Schist hunks
warped as stamps curling off postcards mailed
into the glove compartment. The innumerable
possibilities of number: *down* and *further.*
Amnesiac rock verged on the idea of walls
fallen back from themselves.
Clatter of lithic events.

Stones that begin to people.
Cupped hands offering breadbits saved
from lunch, poppy seeds small as advice.
Granite vocabulary the wind makes easy.
His children call across. In this blank
dazzle that hurts, their faces play
tabula rasa. Cultivated by gales, desk-top
crags leaning further and further
into air. Words that choose
not to hear. The word *love:* the diameter
of Betelgeuse, Marshal Pétain's hat size.
A thin cheeping of arctic conies whose deaf
functional ears seem round as dimes.

Over his lips and face the sandpapering
of upslope weather claims eternity
has never lost sight of him.
The patient voices. Through the country
of rock faces he travels
where nothing but Zeno's paradox works.
Among talus hunks, intricate spider webs
tie one block to another. Low, urgent
voices of stones, insistently gentle
and insane, saying he could
climb back out of here: "Believe us,
this is not where you are."
"It is a word called *home*."
"We are your friends."

Snow like Fan Mail

Early November or barely. We say,
"How charming! So good
to hear again!" The flakes arriving
like fan mail.

To the heat egg. To old
nickel-iron, molten and comfy,
nougat-soft inside.

Word coming down from where
the language has been cold
a long time.
They are writing in about it, each
crystal individually signed.

"Dear Fleshlight," they say, "dear
Cozy! If only we could! Meanwhile
let's keep in touch."

From the heat-lacking countries:
"Dear Rosebud . . ." With January
coming down all over December
we struggle and stare. We bite
our lips and think.

"Dear Brainstone . . ." From
the big black sky
coming down all over. "Dear
Hotrock . . ."

The Bee in the Snow

The left wing delicately
shattered along its tip
veins and branches
finer than sight, out
of the full history of bees.
The snow air swarms
with countlessness
everywhere I look,
on earth and beyond.
As it hums like gravity
pulling the sky down
grain by grain,
I hover one brown husk
and stare
and drift, great
with impossible numbers.

Four Cairns
                    for Les Brill

1

Lichen mouths sipping at stones
and baggy clouds low to the ridge-lines,
old carpenters with blue thumbs.
Setting rock cheek-to-cheek
with the teeter and chink of rock,
what pulls me into form? The shape
of another age felt in this one?
Boulders swagged with growth rings
of heat, and sidereal time
weathering here like wood-grain.

2

Explorers—Amundsen, Scott, living cairn
to cairn piled at the world's ends—
how I pored over journals like that!
The boy's the man, still marking his spot
in the fabulous past of stones.
As each chunk recalls its place
at that seamless ruin of chaos
where everything broken once fit
I'm light blown into reverse,
dwelling whole and immense in a point.

3

Aquinas wrote of even a vegetable soul.
Imagining rocks that remember lost wings
I know they can't, but know
these ptarmigan once were granite. Could stones
be infinitesimally proud of themselves
in us? I think not, but think
there are great winds in the sky,
as each hunk I lift swims me
its long way here, a hive of cells
playing vandal with chance.

4

A bohunk advance
of lighthouse cairns across Bighorn Flats
saying all cairns say the same.
The way we stop at one, listen
to nothing, then move on.
The way hikers touching this cairn
of mine will pause . . . then go.
Knowing I've kept some word,
guessing what word it was.

V

Spring Stuff

and even the clouds go horny look
up there that seagull screwing the chicken
it's rubek the sculptor thwacking away
flailing at stone on wheels
trying to make it with statues that float
and the seeds' big underground guns
firing tree bursts like sight gags
pulled by some cthonic baggy pants comic
and humpty-dumpty the bees
drilling into hollyhocks on the wallpaper
what though last year's bee
his husk his fuzz shroud was nobly borne off
stark by fine-print ants
the golfer drooling nonetheless new
spalding dots like treasure indeed
fresh tees whose water of polished wood
he runs through fingers
the weeds of the field
whose roots have forgotten arthritis
the zoo's pride of winter-coat lions that stir
rehearsing act three of king lear
oh how they once loved it
the used car dealer sneaking into the flock
wearing his fresh lambskin suit
the poet not quite dripped dry
restringing his lyre
for tennis with galway kinnell
and central park its slow its staggery strollers
cuddling their love-knot steps tied up

in circular arrows of blood and again
these clouds simply how bright
becoming all their snowmen could dream
and us too
just drifting
drifting up there with them
light naked perpetual

Turn

By its butt end
wrapped tight with steel wire
so as not to split,
grab the stake.
Heft a flat-sided rock.
Set the hatcheted tip.
Now batter it home.

Years after, haunting
the spot, your knees will whimper.
Go down, both hands roped
behind your back.
Grovel your snout into dirt.
Root at it.
Spit black off to the left.
When your rag tongue
touches oak whiskered soft
from hammering in,
you can bite, nuzzling
back and forth till you jawbone it
out of his heart.

As you carry him home
let his pain
suck into your arms and chest.
The more you stagger
the lighter he grows.
Nights when your dreams

get sick, wake before dawn.
Prowl room to room.
Haunt the foot of his bed
sipping coffee, looking down
into him, into this father of his own
who could become
nearly too heavy to carry.
When morning arrives
let him slip up behind, watching
you shave, waiting his turn.
Call him your son.

April Dawn Snow

Like something incredible
our high rocks under 16 inches
come secretly down in the night!
After my eyes gaped and fell for it
I did half a dozen bad versions
of April Dawn as Snowlight and Kodachrome.
Telling how I'd seen low clouds hang
and coil and mix among Green Mountain
and the gap to Bear Peak, and how
the soft red of their powder shapes
seemed from them, not sun. Plump
colored tents and parachutes
that made me think, "You can't tell
about light this beautiful already."
Which made me try, of course.
The slow churn of rose cloud, "heavy as if
still half snow. Cloud that can barely stir
to lift." I told how near it grazed
the foreground cactus hills. My first
drafts ran on for 3 pages, later ones
shorter. The beautiful I knew
was poison, but adjectives drifted in.
I squeezed them out. I quit where
the mountains cleared and daylight
spoiled the air. Not "Miss Aurora strangled
by a club-footed Phoebus Apollo." Not quite,
but still pure calendar art.
To tell the truth I did bring in how fast
the dawn lost blood. How fir boughs

shuddered when their snow loaves plopped.
How boulders sogged like fallen cake.
How the slant of delicate tint
on our steepest cliffs
collapsed and vomited slush.
What I stressed was how soon a rosy look
turned gully water; how a forest
of pillows blackened to pine by noon.
Closure aimed for something
believable, not what started me off,
like something incredible.
How the naked rock
stood slag gray,
and steaming, and sullen.

Once Before Sunrise

By five-till-seven I'm at the corner
morning fresh for the Boulder City bus,
thinking aloud, "This mountain light is sweet"—
remembering a drink of pebbled water
I had once before sunrise
up near Bear Creek. The sky is deep.
The air is leaping animals in the lungs.

The future, yes, eats the present.
Our planet's always turning.
"These last few months I feel I've wasted."
But at my feet the new moon sails westward,
a bright seed on the sky's blue puddle.

"You can tell that spring is winning—
mornings now are definitely brighter."
The air is mountain water.

"Our meadowlarks near Table Mesa—
maybe they're the voice of the turtle."
The light is leaping animals.
Till the bus comes I'm immortal.

Long's Peak Trail

1

Less than my hand's-breadth deep
the trail soil thumps
under my boot coming down
inches over a time
still monstrous underground.
A tremendous lost weather
in stone.

2

On the East Face of Long's Peak
crags slab and gape.
Runoff trickles cliffs,
finding mistakes. Along
the lower trail I pry into moss
crannies lush as a thumbnail
hothouse—their blossoms
purple and white, pincushioning
tufts with calyxes not even
a raindrop across.
Amidst the pumpkin shambles
of log rot, the plump
blackberry ants.

3

At timberline I wind into
the old dwarf slaughter.
Fir and spruce shoved half over
the edge of life, Gordian knots
of pain, bough tips greened
with their annual millimeters.
The fractured granite
rained blond with iron,
the flame-grained schist—
its undulance
a wind in the stone.
Huge bacon-sided
shards of cliff.

4

My orange tent stutters
and coughs on the same tireless air
persuading these megaliths.
As the brass stove works up
its handful of blowtorch roar,
grotesque hunks boggle above
my canned meat, their forms
hardened short of life,
sulking, miming shock
with a starved troglodytic look.

5

An all-night rain burns wet
sparklers in my ear
or gusts the nylon fly
with static from a first solar flare
carrying black light
into my sleep till I come to—
12,000 feet up in snow,
fooled by the versatility
of water—my mountain gone
soft, each color eaten white.
And settling down
like a final weather
the delicate ice
of cold's last word, simple
as perfect murder
making the earth its egg.

Postcard to Anne

Herding that lawn-mower wheeze
of a Fiat Millecento
back down to Florence
from Altopiano—
or was it Saltina?—
must've taken hours I guess.
What I remember though
was where we got out
near evening
to pick wild iris. Thousands
crazy drunk—swashing their grand
purple swale
along a ditch. Stalks
by armfuls. Blossoms till
our junker was stuffed.
      And down then.
Tooling our rattletrap down
into the angelus bronze,
the city of flowers,
the iris-colored dusk.

Nuisance Caller

Seconds pass. A phone breathing back.
Then a voice, too cheery: "The question is,
where is it you go at night?" "Yin,"
I say, "or Yang, whichever comes first,"
and hang up. My natural history calling
to say our coyotes make half of each deer
the way gravity owns fifty percent of the falls
and, in between beats, the birds.

Pitch dark I open the mailbox
and listen: "You will not be healed,
never amount." The night trees, blueprints
for coal. Staring out through the Milky Way
I catch a shark's grin
flashed from a rainbow of teeth.

Into ancient warfare at 10, my screen
fakes reruns; Iowa herds of patriot
mothers still shelling Viet Nam
with their wombs. I recall shrapnel flecks
that glanced and rang for somebody else,
now ringing for me: "A dash of salt
hit while crossing a bloodstream."

Asleep with one ear, answering
the pillow some part of each night.
Our backyard clods, phoning
the inside word: "The word is by land."

From home, my father says the signal
has always been still
as this pair of spent wings.
Trying not to see what I know
I see them now. They'll be disguised
as eyelids; they'll be candled
by slow green thumbs.

Breathing a Fine Wilderness in the Air

The August sun gone down
we walk the moon
out of the ground, walk Jupiter
up out of the ground
with the moon.

This is the start
the source of desire, having
that one hunger
at heart. A lightness of step
into the place that we know
must always
be part of the distance.

It is how we walk tonight
breathing a fine
wilderness in the air
till we are of that air. And stars
so close
we seem at last among them.